BE THE LOV
SEEK

LEARN TO LOVE YOURSELF, DISCOVER
SELF-WORTH, EMIT POSITIVE ENERGY,
DETECT AND AVOID TOXIC
RELATIONSHIP.

ERICA REILY

Copyright Reserved © 2024

TABLE OF CONTENTS

INTRODUCTION

CHAPTER ONE: UNDERSTANDING SELF-LOVE

CHAPTER TWO: DEVELOPING SELF-LOVE: A PATH
                      TO   INDIVIDUAL SATISFACTION

CHAPTER THREE: EXPLORING THE DEPTHS OF LOVE
                      THROUGH VULNERABILITY

CHAPTER FOUR: CREATING HEALTHY
                      RELATIONSHIPS

CHAPTER FIVE: LETTING GO OF EXPECTATIONS

CHAPTER SIX: PRESENCE AND MINDFULNESS

CHAPTER SEVEN: SELF-REFLECTION AND GROWTH

CHAPTER EIGHT: OVERCOMING BARRIERS

CHAPTER NINE: MOTIVATION AND INSPIRATION

CONCLUSIONS

Review

Dear Appreciated Customer,

I hope you're enjoying the new book you got! I appreciate you choosing to buy my stuff, and I'm happy you did.

I am aware of how valuable your time is and would appreciate any further time you are able to devote to writing a frank assessment. I think customer input is priceless, and I'll use your suggestions to make future products even better.

Please spend a few moments to post a frank evaluation of this book; I would greatly appreciate it. I sincerely appreciate your opinions and feedback, and I would be grateful to hear how you think I might be able to do better.

Thank you for taking the time to give a frank evaluation; I appreciate your dedication to my product.

The very best

Erica Reily

INRODUCTION

The phrase "be the love you seek" highlights the notion that we must first develop the attributes of love and fulfillment inside ourselves before we can expect to find them in other people. The expression implies that rather than depending entirely on outside sources, the kind of love and happy experiences we want should come from within. some essential components of "being the love you seek":

Developing a strong sense of self-love and self-care is the first step towards achieving self-care. This entails having compassion, kindness, and respect for oneself. Taking good care of your mental, emotional, and physical health is an essential step in this process.

Authenticity: A key component of becoming the love you want is staying loyal to who you are. Making true connections with others who value you for who you really are is made possible by embracing and expressing your own self.

Good Attitude and Positive Energy: You can draw in comparable energies from the environment around you by adopting a positive outlook and projecting positive energy. Your relationships benefit from this positivity as well, becoming stronger and more satisfying.

Emotional Intelligence: Having a good understanding of and control over your own emotions as well as the feelings of others helps you form deeper and stronger relationships. To successfully navigate the intricacies of relationships, emotional intelligence is essential.

Generosity and Kindness: Showing others love, kindness, and support without anticipating anything in return is a key component of becoming the love you desire. Generosity starts a beneficial chain reaction that fosters relationships and goodwill.

Establishing Healthy Boundaries: Being the love you want requires that you set boundaries and recognize your own value. It entails being aware of and vocal about your needs while also honoring those of others.

Gratitude: A general feeling of contentment and affection is derived from cultivating a sense of gratitude for the good things in your life. Being grateful for what you have might improve your wellbeing.

Being the love you seek essentially means accepting accountability for your personal fulfillment, happiness, and the caliber of your relationships. It entails a path of self-improvement and self-discovery as well as a dedication to cultivating virtues that lead to a fulfilling and loving existence.

Love for oneself is essential for general health and affects many facets of life. The following are some major points underscoring the significance of self-love:

Mental Wellness:

Resilience: Self-love builds emotional resilience, which makes it easier for people to overcome obstacles in life and recover from failures.

Decreased Stress: Adopting a self-loving attitude might help people feel less stressed because they are more capable of managing pressures in a healthy way when they take care of themselves.

Emotional Health:

Happiness: People are more likely to feel happier and more satisfied with their lives when they put self-love first.

Emotional Regulation: A more stable emotional state and better emotional regulation result from self-love, which entails acknowledging and controlling one's feelings.

Wholesome connections

limits: Building self-love empowers people to set and uphold healthy limits in relationships, which promotes respect and understanding on both sides.

Attracting Healthy Connections: Because they bring a pleasant and satisfied energy to their interactions, people who practice self-love are more likely to draw in and stay in healthy relationships.

Physical Condition:

Better Lifestyle Decisions: People who value who they are are more likely to adopt healthy habits, such as regular exercise, a balanced diet, and adequate sleep.

Reduced Chance of Physical and Mental Health Problems: Making self-love a priority is linked to a decreased risk of mental health conditions as well as some physical health problems.

Efficiency and Success:

Motivation: A strong sense of self-love can work as a catalyst for motivation, encouraging people to confidently pursue their goals and aspirations.

Enhanced Productivity: People are more inclined to devote time and energy to pursuits that further their personal and professional development when they value and take care of themselves.

Enhanced Self-Perception:

Self-love and confidence are intimately related. Self-loving people are more likely to have confidence in their skills and attractiveness.

Positivity in Self-Image: Fostering self-love aids in the development of a positive self-image, which can influence both an individual's perception of themselves and that of others.

Spiritual Development:

Inner Connection: A deeper awareness of one's values, purpose, and spiritual dimensions might result from practicing self-love.

Mindfulness and Presence: Self-love practices like mindfulness can improve spiritual well-being by encouraging an awareness and experience of presence. self-love is a fundamental component of wellbeing that has a good impact on relationships, physical health, mental health, productivity, and general life satisfaction. It is not a selfish or narcissistic quality. Self-awareness, self-compassion, and deliberate attempts to put one's own well-being first are all necessary components of the continual process of developing self-love.

Relationship dynamics and general well-being are impacted by self-love, which has a significant effect on them. Here are a few ways that relationships might benefit from self-love:

Healthy limits; Healthy limits in relationships are more likely to be established and sustained by people who value themselves. They can communicate more clearly and with mutual respect when they are aware of their own wants and boundaries.

Enhanced Empathy; People who take good care of themselves are more likely to be empathetic to others. They are better able to comprehend and relate to their partners' needs and feelings thanks to their emotional intelligence.

Respect for One Another: Respect for oneself is nurtured by self-love, and those who value themselves are more inclined to treat their partners with the same deference. Relationships that are fulfilling and healthy are built on this mutual respect.

Proficiency in Communication: Individuals who place a high value on loving themselves are typically stronger communicators. They are better at listening intently to their partners' worries and honestly communicating their needs and wants.

Resolving Conflicts: People who have a high feeling of self-love are typically better able to resolve problems in a positive way. Rather than acting destructively, they approach conflicts with a problem-solving mentality.

Decreased Dependency; Self-love dissuades reliance on other people for approval and satisfaction. This lessens the possibility of codependent partnerships, preserving the sense of autonomy and personal fulfillment for each partner.

Positive energy and contribution: People who love themselves unconditionally frequently provide a good example for their relationships. When a partner puts their own health first, it might encourage the other person to follow suit, starting a beneficial cycle of growth.

Emotional Balance: Self-love is a necessary component of emotional balance. Emotionally stable people are better equipped to handle the highs and lows of a relationship without putting their spouse through unnecessary stress.

Reaching Intimacy Goals: A strong sense of self-worth can improve a relationship's closeness. People are more inclined to be genuine with their spouse when they feel confident and at ease in their own skin.

Contentment and Gratification: When someone loves themselves, they are more inclined to approach relationships from a place of fulfillment rather than one of needing approval from others. This may result in a more fulfilling and advantageous partnership for both parties.

Although relationships benefit from self-love, it's crucial to remember that healthy partnerships also need mutual respect, clear communication, and a set of core principles. A sound understanding of interpersonal dynamics combined with self-love can lay the groundwork for meaningful and long-lasting relationships.

CHAPTER ONE

UNDERSTANDING SELF-LOVE

The concept of self-love is complex and includes having a healthy and supportive connection with oneself. It entails realizing, respecting, and valuing one's own wellbeing and worth. The following are important elements that help people understand self-love:

Self-Acceptance: Accepting oneself for who you are, flaws and all, without passing judgment. The basis of self-love lies in self-acceptance. It entails accepting oneself and one's flaws as essential components of what makes one special and worthwhile.

Self-Empathy: Being compassionate, understanding, and empathic to oneself, especially when suffering difficulties or setbacks. Treating oneself with the same warmth and consideration as one would a friend is a key component of self-compassion. It encourages fortitude and an optimistic outlook.

Self-Respect: Acknowledging and respecting one's own value and establishing expectations for oneself in terms of treatment. Setting boundaries and refusing to accept relationships or circumstances that jeopardize one's wellbeing are key components of self-respect. It promotes a feeling of honor and empowerment.

Positivity in Oneself: Developing a good self-perception that encompasses one's abilities, character, and physical appearance. A favorable perception of oneself fosters self-assurance and a sound sense of self-worth. It entails realizing one's intrinsic worth and cherishing one's individuality.

Self-Care: Participating in practices and activities that enhance mental, emotional, and physical health is the definition of this term. Making self-care a priority is a sign of self-love. It entails making a conscious effort to take care of and nourish oneself, whether via rest, exercise, or other nourishing pursuits.

Establishing Healthful Boundaries: Setting and conveying boundaries for appropriate interactions, influences, and behaviors. A fundamental element of self-love is establishing sound limits. It entails keeping oneself safe from negative influences and making sure that interpersonal connections are civil and mutually beneficial.

Recognizing Successes: Acknowledging and applauding one's own successes, no matter how minor. A sense of pride and accomplishment is fostered by acknowledging accomplishments. It bolsters the notion that one is worthy and capable of achieving achievement.

Letting Go and Forgiveness: Letting go of judgment of oneself and accepting forgiveness for previous transgressions or perceived inadequacies. Self-love necessitates forgiveness. It enables people to grow from their experiences without clinging to damaging emotions of shame or guilt.

Being mindful and aware of the present moment: Living completely in the now, without thinking about the past or the future. Being mindful fosters self-awareness and enables people to recognize the value of every moment. It improves general wellbeing and lessens needless tension.

Developing an Attitude of Growth: Seeing obstacles and failures as chances for development and learning. growth mindset lies in its ability to cultivate resilience and a positive perspective on personal growth, hence promoting ongoing learning and advancement.

Practice Gratitude: Offering thanks for all the good things in one's life. Expressing gratitude fosters an optimistic outlook, redirects attention from scarcity to plenty, and enhances general welfare.

In conclusion, self-love is an all-encompassing and continuous process that entails accepting oneself, engaging in self-compassion exercises, and giving priority to activities that advance one's own development and fulfillment. It is a fundamental component of developing resilience, wholesome relationships, and a life purpose.

Cultivating a positive and healthy sense of self-worth requires understanding the distinction between self-love and outside validation. An examination of the differences between these two ideas is provided below:

Self-Love:

- *Origin*: Intrinsic and internal, originating from within the individual.

- *Value on its own*: Grounded in recognizing inherent worth and deserving respect, love, and care simply for being alive.

- *Durable and Sustainable*: Independent of external factors, providing enduring and sustainable self-value.

- *Internal Verification*: Validation stems from internal acknowledgment of accomplishments, assets, and positive traits.

- *Put Well-Being First*: Involves prioritizing personal health and happiness through self-care and decisions that enhance fulfillment.

External Validation:

- *Origin:* External, dependent on acknowledgment, appreciation, or acceptance from others.

- *Conditional Authorization*: Relies on meeting external expectations, standards, or societal norms.

- *Modified Subject:* Subject to change and often transient, influenced by external opinions and perspectives.

- *Reliance on Others*: Involves depending on judgments, recommendations, or endorsements from others to feel successful or worthy.

- *Possibility of Insecurity:* Persistent dependence on external validation can lead to feelings of insecurity and low confidence.

Key Differences:

**Origin of Value: **

- Self-Love: Intrinsic and self-recognized.

- External Validation: Dependent on external sources.

**Continuity: **

- Self-Love: Resilient and steady.

- External Validation: Not reliable and subject to shifts.

Self-determination:

- Self-Love: Empowers individuals to control their own well-being.

- External Validation: Potentially dehumanizing, as value depends on uncontrollable external forces.

**Long-Term Effect: **

- Self-Love: Supports sustained emotional fulfillment and well-being.

- External Validation: Offers momentary gratification but lacks lasting depth.

Fostering a more accurate knowledge of self-love also requires dispelling popular myths about it. By clearing up these myths, people can embrace self-love in a more genuine and significant way. The following are some widespread myths regarding self-love, along with debunking explanations:

Misconception: Loving oneself is selfish

Overcoming: Being self-centered or ignoring the needs of others is not indicative of self-love. Rather, the key is to acknowledge your own value and wellbeing so that you can make great contributions to others without compromising your own happiness.

Misconception: Loving oneself is narcissistic

Overcoming: Narcissism and self-love are not the same. While self-love entails a healthy and balanced respect for oneself while retaining empathy and consideration for others, narcissism involves an overwhelming concentration on oneself at the detriment of others.

Ignorance: Arrogance Is Self-Love:

Overcoming: An overblown sense of one's own significance is a component of arrogance. Contrarily, self-love entails appreciating oneself without demeaning others. It's not about being better than other people; it's about developing a healthy connection with oneself.

Misconception: Love for Oneself Is a One-Time Thing:

Overcoming: Learning to love oneself is an ongoing, dynamic process. It calls for constant self-awareness, self-compassion, and deliberate actions. It's a voyage of self-discovery and growth rather than a destination.

Misconception: While Self-Love May Be Easy for Some, It May Be Impossible for Others:

Overcoming: Although the urge for self-love is universal, everyone's journey toward it is unique. It's about development, not perfection. With self-awareness, self-compassion, and deliberate effort, anyone may develop self-love.

Misconception: To love oneself is to overlook flaws:

Overcoming: Loving oneself entails accepting one's flaws as well as talents. It's about treating oneself with respect, compassion, and a dedication to personal development rather than dismissing imperfections.

Misconception: Self-Love Needs Outside Validation

Overcoming: Genuine self-love originates internally and is not reliant on approval from others. Although receiving validation from others can be reassuring, depending only on them to validate you can make you feel insecure. Self-worth can be obtained more sustainably from internal validation.

Misconception: Loving oneself Depends on One's Success

Overcoming: Loving oneself does not depend on reaching goals or benchmarks set by others. It's about realizing your intrinsic value, regardless of your accomplishments, and accepting that errors and failures are inevitable in life.

Misconception: Loving Oneself Is Indulgent

Overcoming: Overindulgence or self-gratification at the price of long-term wellbeing are not aspects of self-love. It entails making decisions that put true fulfillment, health, and happiness first.

Misconception: Love of Oneself Solves Every Issue:

Overcoming: Although self-love is an essential part of wellbeing, it is not a foolproof way to get through every obstacle in life. It enhances other facets of resilience and personal growth, like social support and problem-solving abilities.

People can get over these false beliefs and establish a more genuine and healthy relationship with themselves by being encouraged to have a more nuanced and practical knowledge of self-love.

CHAPTER TWO

DEVELOPING SELF-LOVE: A PATH TO INDIVIDUAL SATISFACTION

In the complex fabric of personal development and wellbeing, developing self-love becomes the luminous thread that runs through all facets of our existence. This path invites us to turn inward and cultivate a very intimate relationship with ourselves—one that is both affirming and compassionate. Let us examine the practices that serve as the cornerstone of this journey of transformation.

Techniques for Developing Self-Love:

Setting out on the journey of self-love requires a number of deliberate actions that reveal our value and open the door to a richer life. It entails doing self-kind deeds, deeds that say to the spirit, "You are worthy." These practices, which range from the straightforward yet profound act of self-care to the deliberate development of positive habits, foster an atmosphere that is supportive of the growth of self-love.

Daily Self-Care Routines: Include quick, regular self-care activities in your everyday schedule. These rituals, which can include anything from a brief meditation session to a brisk walk in the outdoors, can serve as a reminder to yourself that your well-being is important.

Create personal affirmations that are consistent with your goals and guiding principles. These encouraging words act as a daily reminder of your potential and intrinsic value. With determination, repeat these and let their empowering energy seep into your awareness.

Keeping a gratitude journal: Set aside some time every day to recognize and be grateful for the good things in your life. Writing in a gratitude journal helps to cultivate an attitude of appreciation and self-love by turning the focus from what is lacking to what is abundant.

Creating a Good Self-Image:

The canvas on which self-love paints its brightest colors is a positive self-image. It entails changing the story we tell ourselves about who we are, letting go of social norms, and embracing the singular work of art that is "you." Acknowledging and appreciating your uniqueness is more important for cultivating a positive self-image than striving for perfection.

Accepting Your Individuality: Acknowledge and value your special traits, characteristics, and abilities. Accepting your uniqueness helps you develop a positive self-image and a sense of pride in being who you truly are.

Positive Visualization: Envision and become your best self by using positive visualization. Imagine yourself in successful, joyful, and fulfilling situations. Visualization develops into an effective technique for attracting favorable results and strengthening a good self-perception.

Accepting defects: Give up trying to be flawless and accept defects as necessary components of your journey. Recognize that your flaws make you special and offer chances for development and self-compassion.

Growing in Self-Acceptance and Self-Compassion:

The foundation of self-love is self-acceptance and self-compassion, which invite us to treat ourselves with the same love and understanding that we freely give to others. It's about accepting our humanity, with all its strengths and vulnerabilities, and treating ourselves with the care we deserve.

Mindful Self-Compassion: Practice mindfulness to become aware of your thoughts and feelings without judgment. When faced with hardships or setbacks, respond with self-compassion. provide yourself the same care and support you would provide a buddy in a comparable position.

Cultivating Forgiveness: By practicing forgiveness, you can free yourself from the burden of your past transgressions. Recognize that making mistakes is a natural aspect of being human. Continued growth and self-acceptance are made possible by forgiveness.

Unconditional Self-Love: Develop an attitude of unconditional love for yourself by separating your value from approval or constraints from outside sources. Realize that, regardless of your accomplishments or the expectations of society, you are a worthy recipient of love and acceptance.

The following are more doable methods for developing self-love:

1. Embrace Self-Compassion: Be kind to yourself, especially when things are hard. Be the same comfort and understanding that you would provide to a friend going through a hard time.

2. Challenge Negative Self-Talk: Pay close attention to internal conversations, addressing and changing negative ideas into positive, affirming words.

3. Celebrate Achievements, Regardless of Scale: Acknowledge and honor individual successes, no matter how big or small, as this helps to boost self-esteem and cultivate a positive self-image.

4. Establish and Uphold Healthy Boundaries: As an expression of self-respect and dedication to self-care, clearly state and uphold boundaries in relationships and varied circumstances.

5. Practice Mindfulness and now-Moment Awareness: Develop self-awareness and a strong sense of self by living fully in the now, free from worries about the past or the future.

6. Prioritize Self-Care: Give top priority to self-care routines that support mental, emotional, and physical health; these include things like exercise, plenty of sleep, leisure, and hobbies.

7. Grant Yourself Forgiveness: Let go of the weight of previous transgressions by accepting that mistakes are a universal part of self-love and personal growth.

8. Cultivate a Growth Mindset: View obstacles as opportunities for growth and learning, building resilience and a positive perspective on personal development.

9. Surround Yourself with Positivity: Develop connections with people who encourage and support you, creating a social milieu that supports a positive self-perception.

10. Express thankfulness Regularly: Develop an attitude of thankfulness by focusing attention elsewhere and acknowledging and appreciating life's good aspects. This will help you see the bright side of things.

11. Participate in Purposeful Self-Reflection: Set aside time for introspection, thinking back on experiences, values, and objectives to broaden self-awareness and direct personal development.

12. Master the Art of Saying No: Respect your time and energy by becoming adept at turning down offers that could jeopardize your wellbeing.

13. Embrace defects: Recognize and accept defects as essential components of individuality, realizing that while striving for personal development is admirable, perfection is still an unachievable goal.

14. Seek Professional Guidance When Needed: If you need specialized help developing self-love, think about reaching out to coaches, counselors, or mental health specialists.

15. Harness Affirmations and Positive Visualization: Strengthen a positive self-image by using affirmations and visualization techniques. This will help to facilitate a mindset shift that is transformative and reinforce self-love.

Let these practices serve as lanterns, illuminating the way to a deeper connection with ourselves as we negotiate the complex terrain of self-love. We find the grace to appreciate life's most exquisite moments and the fortitude to withstand life's storms in the soft embrace of self-love. The goal of this journey is to reveal the layers of love that have always been inside, not to get to a certain place. Remember that developing a compassionate and loving connection with oneself requires accepting little steps with consistency and patience. The path to self-love is not a sprint.

CHAPTER THREE

EXPLORING THE DEPTHS OF LOVE THROUGH VULNERABILITY

Embracing vulnerability is a transforming and courageous act that entails acknowledging, accepting, and expressing one's actual and authentic self, especially in the face of doubt, imperfections, or potential judgment. This is one of the most important aspects of self-love. It's about letting go of masks and pretenses and allowing oneself to be seen and heard. This is a more thorough examination of accepting vulnerability in the framework of developing self-love:

Genuine Expression of Self:

Revealing Authenticity: Accepting vulnerability means taking off the masks we frequently put on to hide our actual selves. It entails sharing real feelings, ideas, and experiences without worrying about criticism or rejection.

The Courage to Be Inadequate

Letting Go of Perfectionism: When we let go of the unattainable goal of perfection, self-love blossoms. Admitting our flaws and accepting them as parts of what makes us special and human is the definition of embracing vulnerability.

Being Receptive to Feelings:

Expression of Feelings: Being vulnerable is being able to freely express a wide range of feelings, including happiness, sadness, fear, and enthusiasm. It's the readiness to be open and honest about one's feelings with both others and oneself.

Linking Across Our Common Humanity:

Creating Sincere Connections: Being vulnerable serves as a gateway to genuinely connecting with people. Realizing that vulnerability is a common component of the human experience, we open up room for empathy and understanding by being true to who we are.

Self-Caring During Vulnerabilities:

Being Kind to Oneself: Accepting vulnerability is being compassionate toward oneself when you experience difficulties or failures. It is recognizing one's difficulties and extending compassion and understanding in place of self-criticism.

Releasing Your Fear of Being Judged:

Letting Go of the Constant Need for External affirmation and Realizing That Our Worth Is Not Determined by Other People's Opinions: Being vulnerable means letting go of the constant need for affirmation from others. It's an act of self-affirmation that is unaffected by criticism from others.

Handling Uncertainty with Fortitude:

Embracing the Unknown: When we approach life's uncertainties with resiliency and candor, our sense of self-worth is reinforced. By accepting our vulnerability and realizing that we won't always know the solutions, vulnerability enables us to bravely navigate the unknown.

Respecting Limits While Remaining Open:

Maintaining Boundaries while Maintaining Openness: Being vulnerable does not entail oversharing or disobeying restrictions. It entails striking a careful balance between being open and establishing sound limits in order to safeguard one's wellbeing.

Accepting Development and Education:

Seeing Your Weakness as a Strength: Vulnerability is viewed as a source of strength rather than a sign of weakness. It turns into a route for development on a personal level, self-awareness, and the ongoing evolution of one's true self.

Introspection and Self-Revelation:

Unveiling Layers of Self: Adopting a vulnerable stance encourages introspection and a more thorough examination of one's beliefs, aspirations, and anxieties. We embark on a voyage of self-discovery as we develop a deeper awareness of our inner selves.

1. Appreciating the Significance of Vulnerability in Love:
Explanation: A vital component of love is vulnerability, which enables people to openly share their hearts and form sincere bonds. In order to foster closeness and understanding between people, it requires the bravery to communicate feelings, wants, and anxieties.

* Importance:* Vulnerability serves as a bridge in the context of love to strengthen emotional ties between couples and create an atmosphere that is conducive to real, sincere love.

2. Overcoming Fear and Adopting Transparency:

Definition: It is necessary to overcome the fear of being judged, rejected, or emotionally exposed in order to embrace vulnerability. It entails making the conscious decision to be truthful and transparent despite unknowns.

* Importance:* It is freeing to let go of fear and embrace transparency. It enables people to overcome obstacles they have put up for themselves, promoting sincerity and opening doors for real connections, particularly in romantic relationships.

3. Fostering Emotional Resilience:

Explanation: Within the framework of vulnerability, emotional resilience refers to the capacity to overcome obstacles, overcome emotional hardships, and preserve wellbeing in the face of adversity.

* Importance:* People who have developed emotional resilience are better able to accept vulnerability without becoming paralyzed by the dangers. It involves learning coping skills, practicing self-compassion, and having the ability to grow and learn from emotional events.

Traversing Vulnerability in the Love Tapestry:

Accepting vulnerability in the context of love necessitates being open to sharing vulnerabilities and uncertainties in addition to joys and strengths. Here's a closer look at how vulnerability directs the complex path of love:

1. Promoting Genuine Connection:**

Participation: Since vulnerability creates a space where people can communicate their own feelings and thoughts, it promotes genuine connections in romantic relationships. It makes it possible to learn more about one another's inner lives, which fortifies the emotional connection between partners.

2. Establishing Closeness and Trust:

Participation: Being vulnerable is the basis for intimacy and trust. A foundation of trust is established when people feel comfortable enough to be vulnerable with one another, which permits the relationship to grow. When partners reveal their vulnerabilities, intimacy blossoms and a place for emotional closeness is created.

3. Promoting Mutual Development:

Purpose: In love, vulnerability entails a readiness to develop together. It recognizes that both partners are always changing, and sharing vulnerabilities with one another promotes understanding, mutual support, and shared personal growth.

Surmounting Fear and Adopting Transparency:

Vulnerability is frequently impeded by fear, which limits the level of connection that can exist in a loving relationship. It is a transforming process to get over this anxiety and embrace openness:

1. Fostering Self-Assurance:

  Method: To conquer fear, one must cultivate self-worth and confidence. Being able to accept oneself without regard to the perceptions of others creates the foundation for accepting vulnerability with confidence.

2. Expressing Needs and Wants:

Method: It takes efficient communication of needs, desires, and boundaries to embrace openness. It entails speaking from the heart, listening intently, and establishing a secure environment for candid conversation.

Developing Emotional Hardiness: The ability to overcome obstacles and draw lessons from emotional experiences is necessary for navigating vulnerability in romantic relationships.

1. Acknowledging Flaws:

Developing Hardiness: When people accept the flaws in both themselves and their relationships, their emotional resilience increases. It entails realizing that one's weaknesses add to the depth of a relationship rather than detracting from it.

2 Gaining Knowledge from Failures:

Developing Resilience: Resilience is developed via growing and learning from failures. People can treat obstacles as chances for personal and interpersonal growth instead of seeing them as failures.

Love becomes a tapestry woven with strands of transparency, trust, and mutual support in the dance of vulnerability. It's a journey where having the guts to show vulnerability adorns the fabric, weaving together a deep, real, and enduring love.

CHAPTER FOUR

CREATING HEALTHY RELATIONSHIPS

Being the kind of person you want in a partner is essential to establishing and preserving healthy relationships. Investigate these ideas to establish a caring and satisfying relationship:

1. Make Self-Love a Priority: Prior to looking for affection from others, learn to love yourself. Prioritize your well-being, accept your flaws, and value yourself. Meaningful connections are based on a sound self-relationship.

2. Adopt Genuineness: Be sincere and open. By being authentic, you may create a stronger emotional bond and create an environment where communication can flow freely.

3. Excellent Clarity of Communication: Talk honestly and candidly. Listen intently and communicate your wants and boundaries. Understanding and constructive conflict resolution depend on effective communication.

4 Develop Empathy: Gain empathy by being aware of your partner's viewpoint. This base of empathy creates a supportive atmosphere and reinforces the emotional connection.

5. Respect Individuality: Acknowledge and value each other's uniqueness while providing room for personal development and autonomy.

6. Establish Trust: Fundamentally, trust is important. Build trust by being open with one another, being transparent, and keeping your word.

7. Align Values and Goals: Go beyond superficial compatibility to share values and goals in order to foster a sense of togetherness and purpose.

8. Make Quality Time a Priority: Engage your partner thoroughly during quality time. This improves understanding and fortifies the emotional connection.

9. Accept Flexibility: When handling changes and uncertainty, use flexibility. Resilient relationships are a result of both parties' determination to grow together.

10. Practice Dispute Resolution: Learn effective conflict resolution techniques and see disagreements as chances for personal development.

11. Perform Self-Reflection: Consistently consider your actions, words, and contributions to foster personal and interpersonal development.

12. Implement Generosity: Be generous and kind to others. Small acts of kindness and concern for one another foster a positive environment.

13. Maintain Independence: Nurture personal interests and growth for a strong sense of self while developing connection.

14. Show Your Appreciation: Communicate your thankfulness to your partner on a regular basis to create a happy and good relationship.

15. Commit to Growth Together: View the partnership as a growth journey in which you both pledge to advance and help one another.

By living according to these values, you support a happy, caring, and successful partnership. Recall that wholesome relationships include constant work, communication, and sincere dedication to each other's welfare.

More Advice for a Successful Relationship

1. Cultivate Emotional Intelligence: Improve your ability to communicate, empathize, and resolve conflicts by developing your emotional intelligence.

2. Exercise Active Listening: Actively listen to your spouse, encouraging sincere curiosity and reducing miscommunications.

3. Prioritize Quality Communication: For effective expression, concentrate on honesty, clarity, and quality communication.

4. Determine Well-Being Boundaries: To promote mutual understanding and safety, boundaries should be clearly defined and communicated.

5. Celebrate Successes Together: Celebrate and acknowledge each other's accomplishments to strengthen a bond of cooperation.

6. Cultivate Intimacy: Share your vulnerabilities, show tenderness, and spend meaningful time with others to foster emotional intimacy.

7. Cultivate a Growth Mindset: Accept obstacles as chances for development and learning to increase resilience.

8. Nurture Friendship: Create a strong bond between friends by engaging in common interests and fostering a sense of unity.

9. Regularly Express Gratitude: Incorporate appreciation and acknowledgment of efforts into your relationship.

10. Navigate Conflict Constructively: Address disputes collectively, perceiving them as opportunities for knowledge and growth.

11. Assign Equitable Responsibilities: Assign duties equitably to promote a sense of justice and cooperation.

12. Celebrate Individual Identities: Give room for friendships and personal endeavors by celebrating individual identities.

13. Practice Forgiveness: Let go of resentment, accept responsibility for errors, and foster compassion.

14. Adapt to Change Together: Handle life's swings as a partnership, building an adaptable and flexible bond.

15. Seek Professional Support When Needed: If difficulties become too much to handle, think about getting expert assistance, which can provide helpful resources and direction.

16. Celebrate Each Other's Growth: Encourage and commemorate both professional and personal development as means of achieving contentment.

17. Establish Rituals of Connection: Create routines that help people connect, such frequent date evenings or common interests.

18. Exhibit Consistent Love: For a healthy and loving relationship, show affection both verbally and physically on a regular basis.

By incorporating these ideas, you may strengthen the foundation of your relationship and create a space where both partners can thrive and find long-lasting joy.

The Relationship between Healthy Relationships and Self-Love:

Self-love is the foundation of wholesome partnerships. People who develop a strong sense of self-love have a solid foundation of self-worth, confidence, and emotional stability when they join partnerships. They may positively impact the relationship without depending on their partner for approval or fulfillment since they have this internal base.

- ❖ Interdependence, Not Codependence: Instead of encouraging codependence, self-love encourages interdependence. Each partner actively contributes to the partnership while retaining their unique personalities and well-being.
- ❖ Establishing Reasonable Expectations: Self-loving people typically have reasonable expectations for both their spouses and themselves. They realize that being in a relationship is a journey together rather than a means of achieving total personal fulfillment.
- ❖ Vibrant Patterns of Communication: Self-love adds to positive communication habits within the relationship. People who are confident in their own worth and self-esteem are inclined to communicate their wants, needs, and desires honestly, which promotes an open and compassionate atmosphere.
- ❖ Survival under Difficulties: Self-love serves as a safeguard in trying circumstances. Strong self-love practitioners are more resilient and able to overcome setbacks without losing faith in their own value. The relationship's general well-being is positively impacted by this resilience.

Determining Limits and Developing Assertiveness:

A healthy and balanced relationship requires both parties to set and respect boundaries. The limitations of one's needs, comfort zone, and personal space are all defined by boundaries. To be able to properly and honestly communicate one's needs, feelings, and views is to practice assertiveness.

❖ Principles in Focus: Establishing boundaries helps to clarify what is expected of you and what is appropriate in a relationship. This clarity helps both partners negotiate shared areas with mutual respect and lessens the likelihood of misunderstandings.

❖ Preservation of Individuality: Distinct identities are protected by boundaries. They create a partnership in which each partner can flourish separately by allowing them to retain their sense of self and follow their own interests.

❖ Safety for Emotions: Setting limits helps ensure emotional security. People tend to open up emotionally in relationships where they feel valued for who they are, which fosters a safe and trustworthy environment.

❖ Confrontational Speaking: Effective communication is ensured by assertiveness practices. Instead of using hostility or passive-aggression, people can assertively communicate their needs, problems, or desires, encouraging honest communication and problem-solving.

❖

Effective Communication in Relationships:

Healthy relationships are based on effective communication. It entails being aware of one another's viewpoints, listening intently, and communicating ideas and sentiments in a clear and concise manner. Proficiency in communicating fosters intimacy, mutual understanding, and trust.

- ❖ Primary Dynamics: Effective communication begins with active listening. It is important for both parties to make an effort to comprehend one another's points of view without interjecting, assuming anything, or drawing hasty conclusions. By actively listening, miscommunication is decreased and empathy is increased.

- ❖ Use of "I" Statements: Expressing oneself in this way helps one avoid placing blame and promotes personal accountability. For instance, using the phrase "I feel" rather than "You always" encourages a more positive and non-aggressive exchange of ideas.

- ❖ Verification of Emotions: It's critical that we respect and validate one other's emotions. Acknowledging and honoring one another's feelings fosters emotional connection and a supportive atmosphere, even in the face of conflict.

- ❖ Skills in Conflict Resolution: Constructive dispute resolution is a necessary skill for effective communication. When disagreements arise, partners can cooperate to find solutions, make concessions when needed, and see them as chances for mutual development rather than as dangers to the union.

❖ Consistent Visits: Making routine check-ins a habit enables couples to talk about how the relationship is doing, express their thoughts, and handle any issues before they get out of hand. The stability and continued well-being of the partnership are facilitated by open communication.

To sum up, the establishment and maintenance of wholesome relationships are mostly dependent on the interaction of self-love, establishing limits, and skillful communication. People who put their own needs first, speak honestly, and set clear limits create an atmosphere in which both partners may grow emotionally and develop a relationship based on mutual respect, trust, and support.

CHAPTER FIVE

LETTING GO OF EXPECTATIONS; FREEING YOURSELF AND YOUR RELATIONSHIPS

Although they are a normal component of human interactions, expectations can have a big influence on our relationships. Letting go of expectations is a strong process that entails letting go of assumptions, preconceptions, and desired results. Here's a closer look at the idea and how it can change things:

Knowing What to Expect:

❖ Character of Expectations: Mental projections of intended results, actions, or reactions from oneself, other people, or circumstances are called expectations. They may be conscious or subconscious, and cultural, personal, and societal conventions all have an impact.

❖ Aspects, both positive and negative: Unrealistic or poorly stated expectations can cause disappointment, annoyance, and interpersonal conflict, even if some expectations can be constructive, inspiring, and behavior-guiding.

The Negative Consequences of Expectations:

- ❖ Unfulfilled Expectations: Expectations not being fulfilled can cause disappointment, resentment, or irritation. Relationships may suffer and personal wellbeing may be hampered by this emotional intensity.
- ❖ Restricting Expansion: Expectations can stifle the possibility of personal and interpersonal development by limiting people and relationships to preset roles or results.
- ❖ Trained Interaction: Communication hurdles might arise from unspoken or unfulfilled expectations when they take the place of direct and honest discussion.

Embracing Uncertainty:

- ❖ The Liberating Act of Letting Go: Letting go of expectations means accepting uncertainty and realizing that relationships and life are dynamic and that our expectations may not always be met.
- ❖ Autonomy from Authority: People can give up their excessive need for control over other people, themselves, or circumstances when they let go of their expectations. It encourages resilience and adaptation.
- ❖ Situation in the Present: Letting go helps people stop obsessing over the past and start living in the present. It encourages awareness of the present moment and gratitude for the trip.

In Relationships:

❖ Fostering Genuine Relationships: In relationships, letting go of expectations helps people accept their partners for who they are instead of who they think they should be. This leads to the development of genuine bonds.

❖ Minimizing Discord: Realistic expectations can be let go of, which reduces the likelihood of conflict and makes room for candid dialogue and understanding.

❖ Embracing Uniqueness: It promotes acceptance of one another's uniqueness and personal development, understanding that each partner in a relationship is traveling a different path.

Achievable Letting Go Techniques:

❖ Develop Mindfulness: By practicing mindfulness, you can lessen your propensity to linger on your aspirations for the future and remain in the present now.

❖ Open Communication: In relationships, encourage open communication by voicing needs, wants, and worries. Unspoken expectations can be avoided with clear communication.

❖ Reframe Perspective: Change your outlook from one of anticipating certain results to one of openness to possibilities. Instead of viewing obstacles as setbacks, view them as chances for personal development.

❖ Establish Reasonable Goals: Set reasonable aims rather than strict expectations. Think more about the principles and traits you want to exhibit in your relationships than on the results you want to achieve.

❖ Make Flexibility a Priority: Develop a mindset that is adaptable to change and changes as conditions do. Resilience in the face of unforeseen obstacles is fostered by flexibility.

Advantages of letting go:

❖ Improved Well-Being: Releasing oneself from expectations enhances one's mental and physical health by lowering tension, worry, and the psychological damage caused by disappointment.

❖ Integrating Relationships: It does this by encouraging reciprocal support, understanding, and acceptance, which in turn builds stronger and more durable relationships.

❖ Increased Satisfaction: People who let go of irrational expectations frequently report feeling happier in their personal and romantic relationships.

The process of letting go of expectations is ongoing and requires self-awareness, mindfulness, and a dedication to personal development. It is a freeing experience that enables people to value the individuality of both themselves and other people, accept the richness of the present, and build relationships based on mutual understanding and sincerity. Letting go gives one the freedom to face life's challenges head-on with an open heart and a resilient spirit.

Examining Unrealistic Expectations in Love:

Unrealistic Expectations' Nature: - Idealized portrayals in the media, individual experiences, and cultural influences are common sources of unrealistic expectations when it comes to love. These expectations may involve having visions of an ideal spouse, faultless partnerships, or excessively demanding standards of conduct.

Effect on Connections: - Conflict, dissatisfaction, and disappointment can result from having unrealistic expectations. Feelings of inadequacy, bitterness, or discontent might arise when people or relationships don't live up to these inflated expectations.

Principles to Remember

Introspection: Analyzing unreasonable expectations necessitates introspection in order to pinpoint and comprehend their source. It entails considering if these expectations are reasonable or the result of outside influences.

Interaction in Partnerships: It's critical to discuss expectations openly with partners. Setting more reasonable standards for the partnership and fostering understanding are facilitated by talking about expectations and bringing them into line with reality.

Adaptability and Flexibility: People who cultivate flexibility in their expectations are more equipped to adjust to the dynamic nature of relationships. Expectations become more reasonable and enduring when one acknowledges that flaws are a part of the human experience.

Developing an Acceptance Mindset:

Basics of Acceptance: - Acceptance is recognizing and embracing reality as it pertains to oneself, other people, and circumstances. It's about accepting the individuality of every person and situation and letting go of the demand for perfection.

Advantages in Relationships: - Fostering an attitude of acceptance in partnerships fosters empathy, understanding, and unconditional love. People feel appreciated for who they are in this setting instead than being held to unattainable norms.

Realistic Methods:

Acknowledgment of Oneself: Accepting yourself is the first step. Accepting oneself for who you are, flaws and all, promotes a positive self-image and lays the groundwork for accepting others.

Sympathy: Gaining empathy enables people to comprehend and accept, without passing judgment, the viewpoints, experiences, and feelings of others. It improves the emotional bonds between people in relationships.

Creativity: Being mindfully present in the moment and accepting it without passing judgment is encouraged. It lessens the propensity to think back on previous transgressions or have fears for the future.

Appreciating the Beauty of Flaws:

Imperfections Reframed: - Accepting imperfections is seeing them as distinctive features that add to one's uniqueness rather than as defects that need to be fixed. One's imperfections provide oneself and relationships more nuance, character, and authenticity.

Transformational Shifts:

Self-Compassion: - It takes self-compassion to embrace flaws. A loving and caring relationship with oneself is fostered when self-criticism is replaced with kindness and understanding.

Susceptibility: Acknowledging and accepting flaws entails letting oneself be exposed. It entails revealing one's own self, being vulnerable with others, and forming genuine connections.

Growth and Learning: Flaws present chances for development and learning. Believing that errors are opportunities for growth instead of setbacks fosters a resilient and ever-improving mindset.

Impact on Relationships: - Relationships are characterized by greater compassion and forgiveness when people accept the flaws in one other. People can connect more deeply when they accept one other for who they really are—flaws and all.

In short, relationships become healthier, more genuine, and more satisfying when unreasonable expectations are examined, an acceptance-based perspective is developed, and the beauty of imperfections is accepted. It's a path of self-awareness, empathy, and comprehension that improves interpersonal relationships and overall wellbeing.

CHAPTER SIX

PRESENCE AND MINDFULNESS: DEVELOPING THE ART OF LIVING FULLY

Cognizance: The practice of mindfulness involves focusing attention on the here and now without passing judgment. It entails developing an awareness of one's thoughts, feelings, physical sensations, and environment. With its roots in antiquated contemplative traditions, mindfulness has been widely acknowledged for its advantages in enhancing mental health.

Critical Components

1. Attention: To anchor consciousness in the present moment, mindfulness entails purposefully directing attention, frequently through exercises like mindful breathing or meditation.

2. Non-Judgmental Awareness: This method involves paying attention to ideas and feelings without labeling or passing judgment. This attitude of nonjudgmental encourages a sympathetic comprehension of one's experiences.

3. Acceptance: Recognizing that defying reality can result in pain, mindfulness promotes acceptance of the current moment as it is.

4. Breath as an Anchor: In mindfulness exercises, people frequently use their breath as an anchor to help them stay present in the moment.

Advantages:

❖ Reduction of Stress: Research has indicated that mindfulness can lessen stress by encouraging relaxation and an inattentive awareness of stressors.
❖ Enhanced Well-Being: Consistent mindfulness practice has been linked to better emotional control, sharper focus, and an overall higher level of wellbeing.
❖ Increased Resilience: Mindfulness enables people to face obstacles with a calmer, more collected perspective, making them more resilient to setbacks.

Presence; Being fully present and aware of the present moment, whether one is alone or interacting with others, is the state of presence. It entails having a sharper awareness of one's thoughts, feelings, and the people around them.

Critical Components

1. Active involvement: Being present necessitates full attention and active involvement. It entails giving the present moment your whole attention as opposed to dwelling on the past or worrying about the future.

2. Connection: Being in the moment allows for a closer relationship with oneself, other people, and the

surroundings. More genuine and meaningful encounters are made possible by it.

3. Authenticity: Being present entails being authentic, which permits people to express themselves honestly without being unduly impacted by outside expectations.

4. Openness: Being in the present is being willing to interact with the richness of the moment without passing judgment and being open to new experiences.

Advantages:

- ❖ Improved Relationships: By encouraging sincere connections and productive communication, presence improves the caliber of relationships.
- ❖ Enhanced Creativity: Being totally present fosters a more flexible and imaginative way of thinking, which enables people to look at problems from new angles.
- ❖ Heightened Enjoyment: Being present causes people to appreciate life's little joys more since they are more alert and aware of the moment.

Combining Presence and Mindfulness

1. Techniques for Mindfulness in Presence: Mindfulness exercises, like breathing exercises and meditation, are instruments for developing presence. These techniques, which may be incorporated into everyday tasks, teach the mind to concentrate on the here and now.

2. Mindfulness: Present-Moment Awareness: Since paying attention to the present moment is the fundamental component of mindfulness, presence is ingrained in the practice. The two work in harmony to provide a comprehensive strategy for leading a mindful and genuine life.

3. Being Aware During Conversations: Genuine participation, active listening, and a nonjudgmental awareness of the other person are all components of being mindfully present in encounters. This fosters deeper, more sympathetic relationships.

4. Using Mindfulness to Manage Emotions in the Present: Mindfulness exercises help people manage their emotions, which enables them to react to the current situation with more emotional intelligence and poise.

5. Developing a Mindset of Presence: Including mindfulness in daily activities encourages people to approach each moment with intention, attention, and an open heart. This helps develop a presence attitude.

Essentially, presence and mindfulness are related disciplines that enable people to live more authentically, with increased awareness, and with a profound appreciation for the value of every moment. People can see a significant improvement in their relationships and overall well-being by cultivating these attributes.

The Value of Being Present in Relationships: Fostering Well-Being and Connection

1. Creating Sincere Relationships:

❖ Authentic Engagement: Active listening and authentic engagement are necessary components of being present in relationships. It creates a greater knowledge of each other's thoughts, feelings, and viewpoints, building a foundation for meaningful partnerships.

❖ Emotional Intimacy: By fostering an environment where people feel heard, respected, and understood, presence helps to foster emotional intimacy. It deepens the emotional tie between spouses and enhances the overall quality of partnerships.

2. Enhancing Communication:

❖ concentrated Attention: By offering concentrated attention, being present improves communication. People communicate more clearly and reduce misunderstandings when they are totally involved in the conversation.

❖ Non-Verbal Cues: Being present entails being aware of non-verbal clues as well, such as body language and facial expressions, in addition to words. The dynamics of communication are generally improved by this increased awareness.

3. Minimizing Disagreement and Misunderstandings:

❖ Clarity in Intentions: Being present encourages intentions and expressions to be clear. People are more inclined to speak honestly when they are together, which lowers the possibility of misunderstandings that could result in disputes.

❖ Effective Problem-Solving: Being present during difficulties facilitates more efficient problem-solving. By working together to resolve conflicts with a calm, focused approach, partners can strengthen their relationship's resilience.

4. Promoting Emotional Assistance:

❖ Empathetic Presence: An essential element of offering emotional support is being there. Emotionally present partners are able to sympathize with each other's happiness and difficulties, providing support and understanding.

❖ Validation of Feelings: Being present entails accepting and validating one another's emotions without passing judgment. As a result, a safe space is created in which people can express themselves without fear.

5. Generating Satisfying Collective Experiences:

❖ Quality Time: Having a positive impact on shared experiences requires presence. Being present makes the time spent together meaningful and joyful, whether it is through shared activities or deep conversations.

❖ Memory Formation: People who are totally present throughout shared experiences help to create favourable memories. These common experiences lead to a feeling of shared history and deepen the emotional bond.

6. Encouraging Conscientious Decision-Making:

❖ Conscious Choices: Being present involves making decisions in interpersonal relationships. Making decisions with mindfulness entails taking into account how decisions will affect the relationship overall as well as the individuals involved.

❖ Alignment of Values: When couples are in sync and attentive to one another, common interests, aspirations, and shared values can serve as a basis for decision-making.

7. Building a Harmonious Bond with Time:

❖ Appreciating the current Moment: Being in the current moment helps people to enjoy it instead of dwelling on the past or worrying about the future all the time. A more positive engagement with the partnership's evolving path is facilitated by this awareness of time.

❖ Reducing worry: Being present lessens worry brought on the future uncertainty. Couples that have a common commitment to resilience can work through the difficulties of the present.

8. Improving Personal Welfare:

❖ Mindful Self-Care: Being in the moment also means taking care of yourself in the relationship. People who make mindfulness a priority in their personal lives benefit the relationship as a whole.

❖ Stress Reduction: Being present can help reduce stress on an individual and in a partnership. People who practice present-moment mindfulness are able to reduce stress and confront obstacles with more resilience.

9. Achieving Both Physical and Emotional Intimacy:

❖ Mindful Physical Connection: Physical intimacy requires presence. Intimate encounters foster a climate of trust, vulnerability, and shared connection when partners are really present.

❖ Emotional Availability: Being emotionally present is a prerequisite for emotional closeness. A strong and satisfying emotional bond can be developed between partners who are emotionally open to one another.

10. Fortifying Dedication:

❖ Shared Presence as a Commitment: Showing up for the partnership is a sign of commitment. It shows a readiness to devote time, focus, and emotional energy to fostering the relationship.

❖ Navigating Challenges Together: Being there is especially important when things go tough. Present-day partners can work through challenges as a team, building a sense of dedication and unity.

To put it simply, being present in relationships is an effective habit that strengthens the emotional bonds between people. It entails making the deliberate decision to give your all, listen intently, and travel the relationship's path with awareness and sincerity. Beyond one's personal health, being present is crucial for building a relationship based on mutual respect, understanding, and the joy of special times spent together.

Mindful Activities that Promote Love and Attachment: Cultivating Presence in Relationships

Engaging in mindful practices helps strengthen the bond and affection that exist in relationships. These techniques include raising awareness, encouraging a deliberate approach to encounters, and being totally present. To promote love and connection, try these thoughtful activities:

1. Listening with Mind: Allocate a specific period of time to actively listen to your spouse. Keep your eyes open, put away your distractions, and concentrate on comprehending their needs, wants, and words.

Advantages: Mindful listening fosters empathy, a sense of worth, and a better understanding. It improves dialogue and fortifies the emotional connection.

2. Rituals of Gratitude: Thank your partner on a regular basis. Talk about the particular things about them that you like, or the happy times you had. Written notes, group reflections, or spoken affirmations can all be used to achieve this.

Advantages: Having gratitude produces an atmosphere of appreciation, positivism, and reinforcement of good deeds. It fortifies the emotional bond and fosters a sense of acknowledgment.

3. Conscious Conversation: Communicate mindfully by being honest and transparent about your views and feelings. When expressing your viewpoint, use "I" expressions to avoid assigning blame. During conversations, pay attention and be present.

Advantages: Mindful communication reduces miscommunication, fosters emotional security, and provides a secure space for people to voice their wants and worries.

4. Community Mindfulness Exercises: As a couple, include mindfulness exercises in your daily routine. Sessions of meditation, breathing exercises, or even group mindful walks could fall under this category.

Benefits: Shared mindfulness practices promote a sense of unity and shared purpose. It increases the connection by aligning both partners in a focused and present state.

5. Quality Time Without Distractions: Dedicate particular time for quality interactions without distractions. This might be a peaceful time to connect without outside distractions, a weekend retreat, or an evening without technology.

Advantages: Eliminating distractions promotes closer intimacy and connection. It serves to emphasize how crucial the partnership is despite everyone's hectic schedules.

6. Conscientious Touch and Compassion: Be conscious when interacting with others physically. Whether you're giving someone a hug, kissing them, or holding hands, give your whole attention to the feelings and experiences that come with the physical contact.

Advantages: Intimacy between partners is improved by mindful touch, which also fosters a more meaningful and profound bond.

7. Thoughtful Lunch: Take turns eating mindfully. Take note of the food's flavors, textures, and aromas. Talk to each other instead than finishing the meal quickly.

Advantages: Eating mindfully promotes enjoyment and a sense of community. It makes room for meaningful dialogue and the sharing of experiences.

8. Daily Inquiries: Include regular check-ins in which you both discuss your day's highs and lows. This could be a

quick chat before going to bed or at a specific time in the evening.

Advantages: Frequent check-ins reinforce the emotional relationship, foster emotional connection, and offer a forum for mutual support.

9. Resolving Conflicts Mindfully: Handle disagreements with awareness. Prior to responding, stop, breathe deeply, and make an effort to see things from your partner's point of view. To communicate your demands and feelings, use "I" statements.

Advantages: Conscious conflict resolution lessens the severity of arguments, fosters comprehension, and stimulates group problem-solving.

10. Common Mindful Objectives: As a pair, establish conscious objectives. These could be hopes for relationships, personal growth, or group activities that encourage mindfulness.

Advantages: Alignment and purpose are produced by shared mindful goals. By encouraging a common future vision, it fortifies the bond.

11. Intentional Recognition Ritual: Establish a routine in which you each take a moment to express your gratitude to one another. This could be thanking each other out loud, putting messages of appreciation on paper, or just being grateful to each other. Appropriate behaviors are reinforced, a positive environment is fostered, and a loving

and appreciative connection is facilitated via a thoughtful appreciation ritual.

12. Collaborative Digital Detox: Arrange a day or weekend when both spouses give up using electronics as a means of going digital detox. Take advantage of this time to spend with one other, having chats, or going outside.

Advantages: By eliminating outside distractions, a digital detox promotes a stronger connection. It encourages presence in the relationship and makes meaningful in-person interactions possible.

13. Conscious Thoughts: Schedule time for both solo and joint mindful reflections. Think back on the relationship's benefits, your own development, and your shared experiences.

Advantages: Reflecting mindfully improves self-awareness, thankfulness, and a sense of fulfillment in the connection. It promotes a mindful appreciation of the shared adventure.

14. Mindful Bedtime Rituals: Create thoughtful nighttime routines. This could be expressing gratitude, showing affection, or engaging in a quick relaxation technique before bed.

Advantages: At the end of the day, thoughtful bedtime routines foster a sense of community. It encourages sentiments of warmth, safety, and emotional intimacy.

A deeper, more conscious connection can be achieved in your relationship by implementing these mindful techniques. A fulfilling and healthy relationship is built on the love and bond that are nurtured by active engagement, presence, and awareness.

Gratitude Mindset Development: Fostering Happiness and Well-Being

Adopting a thankfulness mentality entails focusing on and valuing life's positive aspects as well as expressing thanks for both minor and major blessings. Numerous advantages exist for mental, emotional, and even physical health when cultivating an attitude of thankfulness. This is a more thorough look at cultivating a thankfulness mindset:

Gratitude: An Understanding

1. Acknowledgment of Blessings: Being grateful is appreciating and acknowledging the good things that have happened to you, your life, and the relationships that have meant something.

2. Change in Perspective: It involves changing one's viewpoint from what could be deficient to what is good and present. This change encourages a gratitude for life's abundance.

Activities to Foster an Attitude of Gratitude:

1. Thanksgiving Diary: Consistently record your blessings in writing. This can apply to relationships, events, self-realizations, or even basic joys.

Advantages: Writing in a gratitude diary encourages introspection, attention, and a deliberate concentration on the good things in life. It supports an optimistic story about an individual's life.

2. Everyday Appreciation Thought: Take some time every day to think about the particular things you have to be grateful for. Either verbal expression or silent contemplation can do this.

Advantages: Regular thanksgiving meditation cultivates an attitude of appreciation for the present. It promotes an optimistic outlook that can penetrate many facets of life.

3. Sending Others Gratitude: Practice Showing thanks to the individuals in your life on a regular basis. Verbal affirmations, handwritten letters, or deeds of compassion can all help achieve this.

Advantages: Gratitude builds bonds between people, creates a supportive social atmosphere, and increases one's sense of interconnectivity.

4. Conscientious Recognition: Take time to mindfully appreciate your surroundings, relationships, or

experiences. Take note of the specifics and relish the good things.

Advantages: Gratitude is experienced more fully when it is expressed mindfully. It promotes being mindful of the kindness and beauty in the moment.

5. Meditation on Gratitude: Include meditation on appreciation in your daily schedule. Concentrate on experiencing appreciation during your meditation, allowing it to seep into your thoughts and feelings.

Advantages: Practicing gratitude meditation lowers stress, fosters inner serenity, and improves general wellbeing. It fortifies the brain circuits linked to happy feelings

6. Challenges of Gratitude: Take part in projects or activities that promote thankfulness. This could be posting daily thankfulness on social media or interacting with a group that promotes thankfulness.

Advantages: Gratitude challenges foster accountability and a spirit of unity in optimism. They promote consistent appreciation practice.

Critical Mentality Turnarounds for Gratitude

Emphasis on Abundance - Change your attention from scarcity to plenty. Acknowledge the wealth of good things in your life, no matter what happens outside of you.

Gratitude for Difficulties - See obstacles as chances for development and education. Look for areas of challenges that advance your own growth.

Awareness of the Present Moment - Practice mindfulness by giving each moment your whole attention. Take note of and delight in the little, happy things of daily existence.

Surrender in Misery - Make an effort to be grateful even in trying circumstances. While it doesn't make problems go away, this does assist in finding things to be grateful for.

Combining Viewpoints - Strike a balance between admitting your shortcomings and keeping an intentional eye on the bright side. Instead of focusing only on the negative, make an effort to find something to be thankful for.

A Gratitude Mindset's Benefits

1. Enhanced Mental Well-Being - Enhanced mental health, including a decrease in anxiety and depressive symptoms, is associated with gratitude. It cultivates emotional fortitude and optimism.

2. Better Connections - Thanking others makes relationships between people stronger. It encourages reciprocity and gratitude in interpersonal interactions.

3. Enhanced Adaptability - Having an attitude of thankfulness makes one more resilient to setbacks. It aids

people in navigating challenges from a more upbeat and hopeful standpoint.

4. Advantageous Physiological Impacts - Gratitude exercises have been linked to advantageous physiological outcomes, such as stronger immunity, less stress, and better sleep.

5. Higher Level of Life Contentment People who have an attitude of appreciation frequently express greater levels of life pleasure. They frequently concentrate on the good things in life, which adds to a general sense of fulfillment.

6. Incentives for Generosity - Being grateful can inspire people to perform deeds of generosity and kindness. Having a grateful mindset is frequently associated with the desire to give back and improve the lives of others.

Building Gratitude into Everyday Living

1. Gratitude Ritual in the Morning - Start each day by thinking about a few things for which you are thankful. This creates a good vibe for the rest of the day.

2. Reminders of Gratitude - Make notes to remind yourself to stop and give thanks throughout the day. This could be a quick time for introspection during intervals or changes.

3. Before Going to Bed - Conclude your day by recognizing and celebrating your victories. This can be accomplished by journaling your appreciation in writing or by introspection.

4. Surrender in Difficulties - When things are hard, make a conscious effort to find things to be thankful for. This may assist in altering your viewpoint and reaction.

5. Expressing Thanks as a Family - Encourage your family to practice thankfulness. At dinners or get-togethers, encourage family members to express their gratitude for what they have.

6. Milestone Celebration - Set aside time to commemorate individual and group accomplishments. Think back on the trip and be thankful for the advancements made.

Having a grateful mentality is a continuous process that calls for deliberate awareness and constant effort. Gratitude may be incorporated into many areas of your life to create a positive feedback loop that improves the quality of your relationships and your overall wellbeing.

CHAPTER SEVEN

SELF-REFLECTION AND GROWTH: NURTURING PERSONAL DEVELOPMENT

One of the most effective tools for personal development is self-reflection. It entails deliberate reflection, introspection, and evaluation of one's ideas, emotions, deeds, and experiences. People learn about their values, goals, areas of strength, and opportunities for growth through self-reflection. Here's a closer look at the relationship between introspection and development:

Having a working definition of self-reflection: The process of looking inside to comprehend oneself better is called self-reflection. It entails investigating ideas, feelings, actions, and experiences with an inquiring and accepting attitude.

Aim: Enhancing self-awareness is the main goal of self-reflection, which promotes both professional and personal progress. It offers the basis for a life that is deliberate and attentive.

Important Elements of Self-Reflection

➢ Concepts and Ideas: Analyze your ideas and opinions, considering where they came from and how they affect your feelings and behaviors.

➢ Emotional Awareness: Recognize and comprehend your feelings. Examine the underlying causes of particular emotional reactions and how they affect judgment.

➢ Characteristics: Identify patterns of conduct that are repeated. Consider whether these tendencies support your aims and values or if they get in the way of your personal development.

➢ Priorities and Values: Make your priorities and essential values clear. Think about whether the decisions and behaviors you make are consistent with these core facets of who you are.

The Significance of Self-Reflection in Personal Development

➢ Determination of Advantages: It's possible to recognize and appreciate your strengths through self-reflection. Acknowledging your skills gives you the confidence to use them for both career and personal success.

➢ Awareness of Developing Areas: Sincere introspection reveals areas in need of development. One of the most important steps in developing oneself is seizing these chances for improvement.

- Aligning and Setting Goals: Setting goals is influenced by introspection. You can develop objectives that are relevant and in line with your desires and contribute to your overall progress by having a clear grasp of your beliefs.

- Improved Judgment-Taking: You can better understand your values and priorities by reflecting on yourself. Making deliberate and well-informed decisions is aided by this clarity.

- Enhanced Adaptability:** Being reflective helps you become more flexible. You become more adaptable, taking lessons from past mistakes and changing course when necessary.

Effective Self-Reflection Techniques

- Journaling: To keep track of your thoughts, feelings, and experiences, keep a reflective notebook. Review and examine your entries often in order to spot trends and revelations.

- Meditation with mindfulness: Maintaining awareness of your thoughts and feelings requires practicing mindfulness. Effective self-reflection and increased self-awareness are supported by mindfulness.

- Input Seeking: To obtain outside viewpoints, ask for input from others. Positive criticism can provide insightful information that self-reflection alone might not be able to provide.

- Consistent Visits: Plan to check in with yourself on a regular basis. Take advantage of this time to evaluate your overall level of contentment with life, your progress toward your goals, and your general state of well-being.

➤ Review of the Goal: Review your objectives on a regular basis to see if they are still applicable. Make any necessary adjustments to reflect your changing goals.

Getting Past Self-Reflection Obstacles:

➤ A Fear of Self-Discovery: Some people could be afraid of what they find out about themselves. It's critical to approach introspection with self-compassion, realizing that growth necessitates accepting both one's talents and places in need of development.

➤ Overanalyzing: Egocentric thinking can impede the efficacy of introspection. Strike a balance between reflection and action by concentrating on takeaways rather than being mired in pointless analysis.

➤ Resistance to Change: During self-reflection, identify and address any resistance to change that may surface. Accept the fact that moving beyond of one's comfort zone is often necessary for advancement.

Including Reflection in Everyday Activities

➤ Daily Schedule: Set aside some time in the morning to reflect on yourself. Think about your daily priorities and how they relate to your long-term objectives.

➢ Evening Reflection: At night, consider your day. What was successful? What difficulties did you encounter? What did you discover? You can include everyday experiences into your growth path by engaging in this activity.

➢ Relax and Inhale: Include breaks in your schedule all throughout the day. Breathe deeply a few times and consider your goals, feelings, and mental condition right now.

➢ Consistent Review Meetings: Set up recurring review sessions, perhaps weekly or monthly, to evaluate your progress and modify your plans and objectives as needed.

Adopting a Growth Mindset

➢ Receptivity to Information: Having a growth mindset means being receptive to new experiences, obstacles, and criticism. Adopt a perspective that views failures as chances for growth and development.

➢ Flexibility: Develop flexibility by realizing that progress frequently necessitates adjusting to shifting conditions. Be prepared to modify your plans and objectives as necessary.

➢ Marking Advancement: No matter how little your progress is, acknowledge it. Recognize and value the efforts you've made to achieve your objectives.

Introspection and Social Connections

- ➤ Comprehending Interactions: Incorporate introspection into your relationships with other people. Think about the effects your behavior and communication style have on your relationships.
- ➤ Developing Empathy: Thinking back on your personal experiences improves empathy. It makes it easier for you to comprehend the thoughts and feelings of other people, which promotes deeper relationships.
- ➤ Resolving Conflicts:** Conflict resolution benefits from a contemplative mentality. Understanding your personal triggers and reactions will help you approach confrontations with a more productive and empathic mindset.

Seeking Guidance and Assistance for Development

- ➤ Coaching and Mentoring: Participate in coaching or mentoring relationships to obtain outside advice. Mentors and coaches can assist your growth process and offer insightful viewpoints.
- ➤ Community Engagement: Make connections with communities or like-minded people who are committed to personal growth. Talking to people about your experiences and learnings can help you reflect on yourself more deeply.

A Mindset of Lifelong Learning

- ➤ Inquisitiveness: Have an insatiable curiosity for life and a desire to learn. Accept new experiences and challenges as chances for personal development.

➢ Continuous Development: Develop an attitude of ongoing improvement. See every day as an opportunity to grow, change, and improve as a person.

A dynamic and continuous process, self-reflection is the cornerstone of personal development. Through regular intentional introspection, people can develop resilience, realize their full potential, and deal with life's challenges with more self-awareness and intentionality. Over the course of a lifetime, the path of self-reflection and growth is an incredibly fulfilling and intimate inquiry.

The Function of Self-Reflection in Personal Development

Applying Lessons from Love's Past and Ongoing Development as a Basis for Lasting Love

1. Using Self-Reflection to Spark Personal Growth:

Explanation: The intentional and conscious analysis of one's ideas, feelings, actions, and experiences is known as self-reflection. It offers insights into many facets of one's life and acts as a potent stimulus for personal growth.

Critical Components:

➢ Awareness: Self-reflection fosters self-awareness, which enables people to comprehend their priorities, values, and driving forces. The process of identifying patterns. Analyzing prior events presents a chance for personal development by pointing out patterns in feelings, ideas, and actions.

➤ Goal Alignment: People can ensure a more meaningful and purposeful pursuit of personal development by aligning their goals with their basic beliefs through self-reflection.

Relation to Individual Growth

➤ Developing Social and Emotional Skills: By promoting a better awareness of one's own emotions and the capacity to manage them, self-reflection raises emotional intelligence.

➤ Switching with the Times: Self-reflection provides insights that help people become more adaptable, allowing them to overcome obstacles in life and change with the times.

➤ Building Up Resilience: Self-reflection fosters resilience, which enables people to overcome obstacles and view challenges as opportunities for personal development.

2. Drawing Lessons from Love's Past

Value of Introspection in Love

➤ Recognizing Relationship Dynamics: In the context of love, self-reflection entails figuring out how one fits into relationship dynamics, spotting communication patterns, and evaluating how one's history has affected one's present connections.

- Identifying the Types of Attachments: People might investigate their attachment styles and how they might affect how they view intimacy and love. A better understanding of attachment styles leads to more positive dynamics in relationships.
- Growing from Errors: Relationships in the past have taught us important things. Self-reflection enables people to identify relationship problems at their core, learn from their mistakes, and make wise decisions in their future relationships.

Important Considerations for Learning from the Past

- Determining Patterns in Relationships: Thinking back on previous relationships can be a useful tool for spotting patterns, both good and bad, and can help break negative cycles.
- Explaining Expectations for a Relationship: Through introspection, people can make their wants, boundaries, and expectations in love clear. This clarity promotes healthier ties and improves communication.
- Evaluating Individual Development: In the context of love, evaluating personal progress entails recognizing areas for improvement, appreciating accomplishments, and realizing how experiences shape continuing development.

3. Ongoing Development as the Basis for Lasting Love

A Mindset Focused on Growth in Love

➤ Together, Accepting Change: In enduring love, both parties pledge to advance individually and as a group. Having a growth-oriented mindset entails being flexible, picking up lessons from shared experiences, and developing both personally and as a pair.

➤ Common Objectives and Principles: Partners who are dedicated to ongoing development have values and aims that are in line. They provide a basis for encouragement and growth from one another and support one another's goals.

➤ Building a Dynamic Connection:** A partnership built on constant development is robust and vibrant. Together, partners grow and change as they embrace difficulties, adjust to new stages of life, and thrive in an environment of mutual learning.

Putting Continual Love Growth into Practice:

➤ Open Communication: Partners who are dedicated to growth have open discussions about their respective and common objectives. This openness promotes comprehension and aids in adjusting to aspirational shifts.

➤ Encouraging Personal Development: Both partners proactively support and foster the other's personal growth. This could entail exploring new interests, going back to school, or adjusting to a job shift.

➢ Collaborating to Learn: Couples that are dedicated to lifelong learning actively look for possibilities for shared education. This can entail going to workshops, reading aloud, or taking part in activities that foster mental and emotional development.

Advantages of Constant Love Development

➢ Newfound Excitation: A dedication to development keeps the partnership lively and new. Discovering new facets of one another and oneself brings delight to partners.

➢ Creating Hardiness: Growth that never stops encourages resiliency in the face of difficulties. When partners approach challenges with a common attitude of growth and adjustment, the basis of their love is strengthened.

➢ Integrating Link: Partners develop deeper connections as they mature. Mutual understanding, support, and encouragement are the foundations of the link formed by shared developmental experiences.

Self-reflection is a guiding light on the path to love and personal growth. It makes clear the way to self-awareness, makes it easier to draw lessons from the past, and cultivates a growth-oriented perspective on love. Couples can build a strong and vibrant foundation for love that is fueled by their ongoing evolution as people and as a relationship, mutual support, and the constant possibility of personal development. Accepting the transformational potential of introspection and ongoing development establishes the foundation for a love that not only endures but grows stronger with time.

CHAPTER EIGHT

OVERCOMING BARRIERS: HANDLING DIFFICULTIES FOR INDIVIDUAL DEVELOPMENT AND ACHIEVEMENT

There are many difficulties in life, and conquering them is essential to success and personal development. Resilience and success depend heavily on one's capacity to overcome obstacles, whether they arise in the workplace or in personal life. Here's a closer look at the idea of conquering challenges:

1. **Knowing what to look for:** Barriers or difficulties that prevent achievement or advancement are called obstacles. They may show up as unexpected events, constraints on oneself, or outside conditions, among other things. There are two types of obstacles: internal ones that involve fear, self-doubt, or limiting beliefs, and external ones that include cultural expectations or financial limitations.

2. **The Significance of Surmounting Difficulties**:

Developing Resilience: Overcoming challenges increases resilience, or the capacity to recover from setbacks. It gives the resilience to take on new difficulties.

Individual Development: Difficulties present chances for personal development. Overcoming challenges frequently entails picking up new knowledge, views, and abilities.

Reaching Objectives: A goal's pursuit is inevitably fraught with difficulties. Overcoming them successfully increases a person's sense of accomplishment and moves them closer to their goals.

3. Standard Life Obstacles:

Fear of Failing: The dread of failing can impede development. Reframing failure as a springboard for achievement and education is necessary to overcome this barrier.

Insufficient Resources: Limited resources can provide serious difficulties, whether they be in the form of money, time, or experience. In these kinds of scenarios, creativity and ingenuity are crucial.

Self-Talk That Is Negative: Internal barriers can be rather strong and include self-limiting ideas and negative self-talk. It takes developing a positive outlook and increasing self-confidence to overcome difficulties.

External Pressures: External barriers may include duties to one's family, peer pressure, or societal expectations. In order to navigate these, one must establish limits and adhere to their moral principles.

4. Methods for Getting Past Challenges:

Positivity Mentality: It is essential to cultivate an optimistic outlook. This entails keeping an optimistic attitude and rephrasing obstacles as chances for development.

Aim Setting: Well-defined objectives offer a path through challenges. The trip becomes more attainable when bigger objectives are divided into smaller, more doable activities.

Flexibility: One important tactic in the face of change is to be flexible. People that possess flexibility are able to modify their strategy when faced with unforeseen obstacles.

Skills for Solving Problems:** Gaining proficiency in problem-solving techniques improves one's capacity to overcome challenges. This entails assessing problems, coming up with fixes, and putting those fixes into action.

5. Acquiring Knowledge from Failures:

Accepting Failure as a Chance to Learn: Consider failure as a valuable lesson rather than the end result. Examine what went wrong, draw conclusions, and use those conclusions in your future work.

Cultivating Resilience: Overcoming adversity is the foundation of resilience. Think back on previous difficulties and recognize the resilience acquired from overcoming hardship.

Adjusting techniques: Adapting techniques is a necessary part of learning from failures. If a specific strategy hasn't produced the expected outcomes, be prepared to adjust plans and explore different approaches.

6. Overcoming Challenges in Workplace Environments:

Successful Interaction: It is essential to communicate effectively in a professional setting. Creative solutions can arise by clearly communicating problems, getting input from others, and working together with coworkers.

Ongoing Education: Sectors change, and it's important to stay informed. Adopt an attitude of perpetual learning to surmount obstacles brought about by changes in the industry or in technology.

Collaboration and Networking: Developing a strong professional network and working with others can offer a variety of viewpoints and tools to effectively address problems.

7. Overcoming Personal Development Obstacles:

Self-Evaluation: Identifying personal obstacles is facilitated by regular self-reflection. Overcoming obstacles begins with recognizing one's areas of strength and growth.

Determining Individual Limitations: Setting up appropriate limits is crucial for personal development. To prevent burnout, it entails setting boundaries and giving self-care first priority.

Looking for Assistance: Seeking assistance from mentors, friends, or family can offer insightful viewpoints and motivation during trying times.

8. Resilience's Function in Overcoming Difficulties:
The capacity to overcome hardships, obstacles, or setbacks is resilience. It entails responding constructively to adversity and hardship.

Creating Hardiness: Overcoming challenges is the foundation for developing resilience. Resilience is enhanced by accepting obstacles with a growth-oriented mindset.

Meditation Techniques: Meditation and other mindfulness techniques can increase resilience by encouraging emotional control and present-moment awareness.

9. Retaining Drive:

Defining Objectives: Review and define your professional or personal goals on a regular basis. Setting and achieving specific goals gives one direction and motivation, which facilitates overcoming setbacks.

Celebrating Small Wins: Along the road, recognize and commemorate your little successes. Acknowledging any kind of progress, no matter how small, increases drive and strengthens optimistic thinking.

Showing Off Success: Using visualization techniques, one imagines overcoming challenges with success. Confidence and motivation can both be increased by this mental practice.

10. Overcoming Relationship Challenges:

Effective Communication Techniques: To overcome relationship roadblocks, effective communication is essential. Having an open and sincere conversation facilitates problem solving.

Compassion and Perception: Relationships that are characterized by empathy and understanding are supportive. Partners who are aware of one another's viewpoints can cooperate to solve problems.

Resolving Conflicts: It's crucial to acquire effective dispute resolution techniques. Open communication about disagreements and the pursuit of win-win solutions improve relationships.

Overcoming hurdles is a necessary component of the human experience, and overcoming obstacles is a key to success and personal development. A happy and meaningful life is facilitated by the capacity to overcome challenges with perseverance, adaptation, and an optimistic outlook, whether in interpersonal relationships, career endeavors, or personal growth. Every challenge offers a chance for growth, self-awareness, and the ongoing development of one's abilities. Overcoming barriers and using them as stepping stones to success turns them into forces for personal development and accomplishment

Typical Obstacles on the Path to "Be the Love You Seek"

1.Love and Worth for Oneself:

Problem: Overcoming anxieties, self-doubt, and a low sense of self-worth can be quite difficult. Negative self-perception might be influenced by outside factors, memories from the past, or social expectations.

Actions: Focus on your personal strengths, confront your negative beliefs, and cultivate self-compassion. Take care of yourself and, if necessary, seek expert assistance.

2.Susceptibility to Rejection and Fear of It** -

Difficulty: Being vulnerable and exposing oneself to others can be frightening. Being the kind of person one wants to be and fostering a genuine relationship might be impeded by the fear of being rejected or judged.

Actions: Increase vulnerability gradually, begin with people you can trust, and work on accepting who you are. Recognize that being vulnerable can be a strength and that it's essential to forming deep connections.

3. Associations and Luggage:

Difficulty: Emotional baggage and previous relationship patterns might affect how people connect now. Having unresolved conflicts or traumas might make it difficult to build positive relationships.

Actions: Seek treatment to address unresolved issues, engage in self-reflection to spot patterns, and make a conscious effort to interrupt bad relationship cycles.

4. Difficulties in Communication:

Difficulty: Relationship formation and maintenance require effective communication. Communication breakdowns, miscommunications, or trouble expressing feelings can all lead to communication barriers.

Actions: Increase your ability to communicate by being aggressive, listening intently, and clearly expressing your emotions. Get input from people to find out how your communication style affects them.

5. Keeping Independence and Interdependence in Check

Difficulty: It might be difficult to find a balance between connection and independence. It might be difficult to strike a balance between preserving individualism and creating a shared existence.

Actions: Clearly state expectations, set clear boundaries between you and the other person, and promote candid discussion about your needs and your relationship's common objectives.

Methods for Overcoming Barriers and Delays:

1. Awareness and Self-Reflection: Think about your own values, beliefs, and actions on a regular basis. Become more self-aware to recognize trends and stressors. To overcome barriers, one must first have an understanding of oneself.

2. Vision and Goal Setting: Make it clear what kind of relationship and affection you're looking for. Establish attainable objectives for your own development and the dynamics of your relationships. Make a picture of the kind of love you want to be.

3. Awareness of the Present Moment and Mindfulness: Remain present in your relationships and interactions by engaging in mindfulness practices. Making better decisions and forming stronger connections is facilitated by being cognizant of one's thoughts, feelings, and behaviors in the moment.

4. Developing Emotional Intelligence: Develop your emotional intelligence to better comprehend, control, and relate to others' feelings. Deeper connections and improved communication are fostered by emotional intelligence.

5. Cultivating Resilience: Build resilience so that you can overcome obstacles. Recognize that obstacles are an

inherent aspect of relationships and life. Instead of seeing setbacks as failures, put your attention on learning and development.

6. Looking for Assistance and Direction: Never be afraid to ask friends, family, or experts for help. A therapist or counselor can offer insightful advice and direction when negotiating obstacles in relationships and personal development.

7.Ongoing Education and Flexibility: Have a growth mentality and be open to lifelong learning. Be willing to modify your strategy in light of criticism, life lessons, and fresh perspectives. A willingness to learn and flexibility are two traits that support personal growth.

8. Determining and Upholding Boundaries: Establish limits and have clear communication in relationships. Honor other people's limits as well. Healthy limits offer a sense of safety and ensure mutual respect.

9. Forgiveness and Letting Go: Practice forgiveness, both towards others and oneself. Holding onto grudges or previous mistakes can limit personal growth and harm relationships. Letting go enables for healing and forward progress.

10. Reflecting Advancement: Celebrate and acknowledge minor accomplishments and turning points in your personal growth. Acknowledge your accomplishments and

seize these opportunities to spur on additional development.

11. Ongoing Feedback and Communication: Encourage candid dialogue in interpersonal relationships. Check in with your spouse and yourself on a regular basis. Seek and offer helpful criticism to make sure that the other person feels heard and understood.

12. Developing an Upbeat Attitude: Develop an optimistic outlook by reinterpreting obstacles as chances for development. Instead of focusing on your limitations or past failures, consider your opportunities and talents.

13. **Compassion and Empathy:** - **Plan:** Develop compassion and empathy for other people as well as for yourself. Recognize that each person is traveling a unique path, and that empathy can deepen bonds and promote understanding.

14. Choosing a Long-Term Viewpoint: Take a long-term approach to relationship building and personal development. Recognize that development is an ongoing process and that growing together over time is the cornerstone of enduring love.

By applying these techniques to your quest to "be the love you seek," you establish a foundation for conquering challenges, encouraging development, and establishing deep connections with people.

CHAPTER NINE

MOTIVATION AND INSPIRATION FOR "BE THE LOVE YOU SEEK" JOURNEY

Starting the path to "be the love you seek" entails developing love, compassion, and understanding within of oneself. In this life-changing process, motivation and inspiration are essential components that influence how you view relationships, self-love, and personal growth.

1. Get Inspired to Be the Love You Desire:

Outlining Characteristics and Values: You are inspired to list the principles and attributes you look for in a partner. It promotes self-reflection to find the parts of love that speak to your true self.

Taking Up Self-Love: Inspirational experiences have the power to help people realize how important it is to love themselves. It inspires you to be kind and compassionate to yourself, just as you would like to be treated in a love relationship.

Growing from Experience: Narratives of compassion, love, and personal development from others can act as beacons of hope. They show how it is possible to become a source of love for others.

Linking with Elevated Principles: Your quest to embody love might be aided by looking for inspiration from higher values, whether they be philosophical or spiritual. It could entail making a connection with values such as empathy, compassion, and unconditional acceptance.

2. Inspiring to Be the Love You Desire:

Determining Your Own Objectives: Setting specific objectives to match your behavior with the love you want to live out loudly becomes motivating. These objectives could be developing stronger bonds, boosting self-love, or increasing communication.

Developing Good Habits: The development of healthy behaviors that help you become the person you want to be loved is fueled by motivation. This could be saying positive things aloud every day, being grateful, or doing good deeds.

Guiding Personal Development: Your motivation for personal development becomes your driving force. It strengthens your ability to bounce back from setbacks and gets you through the inevitable ups and downs of becoming a more loving person.

Developing Social and Emotional Skills: Emotional intelligence is developed through motivation, which helps you recognize and control your feelings. Consequently, this improves your ability to react to people in a loving and compassionate manner.

3. How Inspiration and Motivation Interact in Partnerships:

Motivating Positive Dynamics in Relationships: Aiming for and imagining better relationship dynamics might be sparked by inspirational occasions. Your motivation then spurs you to take proactive steps to cultivate such dynamics.

Encouraging Good Interactions: Your relationships are guided by your motivation, which promotes constructive interactions and communication. It encourages you to interact with people in a more patient, understanding, and encouraging manner.

Models of Relationships as Inspiration: You may be inspired to imitate those traits in your own relationships by looking for positive relationship models as role models. This could include reading relationship books, watching happy couples, or picking the brains of mentors.

4. Difficulties and Overcoming Obstacles:

Overcoming Obstacles with Inspiration: When attempting to live out the love you desire, inspiration can be a source of courage. It sustains you by serving as a reminder of the principles and values that drive your journey.

Inspiration as Hardiness: During setbacks, motivation serves as a building block for resilience. It inspires you to grow from setbacks, modify your strategy, and carry on striving to be the love you want.

5. Ongoing Development and Adjustment:

Inspiring Evolution: You feel as though you are always evolving when you are inspired, and this pushes you to discover new aspects of love and yourself. It arouses a desire for continuous development and education.

Motivated Adaptability: Motivation guarantees that you will continue to be flexible while traveling. It inspires you to modify your tactics, establish fresh objectives, and welcome change as you progress in your pursuit of becoming the love you desire.

6. Appraisal of Oneself and Fresh Inspiration:

Motivated by introspection: Frequent introspection serves as a creative catalyst. It enables you to evaluate your development, recognize your successes, and pinpoint areas in which you still need to grow.

Incentives for Ongoing Self-Work: Motivation is what keeps one committed to ongoing self-improvement. It encourages you to devote time and energy to pursuits that advance your interpersonal and personal growth.

7. Internal Motivators and External Influences:

Keeping Internal and External Motivation in Check: Although the path can be started by outside factors like motivational tales or uplifting role models, internal drive is necessary for long-term change. It requires a dedication on a personal level to consistent work and development.

Integrating Motivational Principles: Motivation is the energy that absorbs the virtues and ideals that are influenced by outside sources. It turns outside inspiration into a motivating force that directs your day-to-day decisions and actions.

Within the framework of "being the love you seek," motivation and inspiration are entwined forces that direct your attitude to self-love, relationships, and personal growth. They interact in a way that is dynamic and inspires your goals and drives your behavior in your quest to live a life filled with the love you deserve.

Inspirational Phrases:

1. "To love oneself is the beginning of a lifelong romance." - Oscar Wilde

2. "Your task is not to seek for love, but merely to seek and find all the barriers within yourself that you have built against it." - Rumi

3. "The more you love yourself, the less nonsense you'll tolerate." - Unidentified

4. "Your heart is filled with so much love. Take a little for yourself." - R.Z.

5. "Love yourself first, and everything else falls into line." - Lucille Ball

6. "The most powerful relationship you will ever have is the relationship with yourself." - Maraboli, Steve

7. "You are worthy of the love you keep trying to give to everyone else." - Unidentified

8. "Set boundaries because you love who you are. You have limited time and energy. How you use it is up to you." - Unidentified

9. "An empty cup cannot be used to pour from. Prioritize your own well-being." - Unidentified

10. "Your relationship with yourself sets the tone for every other relationship you have." - Holden Robert

Affirmations to Help You Be the Love You Desire:

1. I start by loving myself completely because I deserve love.

2. I easily draw love into my life because my heart is open.

3. I accept my deservingness of love and let go of any negative self-beliefs.

4. I am a wellspring of kindness, love, and compassion.

5. I'm becoming into a more loving, optimistic version of myself every day.

6. I deserve to be loved just as much as I love other people.

7. I've made the decision to let my inner love shine forward.

8. I draw polite and caring connections into my life.

9. I am able to show and receive love in positive, healthy ways.

10. The basis of all my relationships is my love for myself.

11. I draw loving individuals into my life because I am a magnet for love.

12. I am worthy of love, complete, and sufficient.

13. I give up my need for validation and embrace my true self.

14. For myself and everyone around me, I choose love, joy, and peace today.

15. I am a love vessel, and I have a great influence on everyone I come into contact with.

As a constant reminder of your resolve to embody the love you desire in your life, repeat these affirmations frequently.

CONCLUSION

ACCEPTING THE SELF-LOVE JOURNEY

We explored the depths of self-love in this enlightening discussion, offering a thorough manual for anyone looking to take this liberating path. Below is a condensed overview of the main ideas covered:

The foundation of one's own well-being is self-love, which entails acceptance, compassion, and a close bond with oneself. It is a purposeful, continuous practice that calls for self-awareness and a dedication to attending to one's own bodily and emotional needs. Self-love is a basic requirement for creating wholesome relationships and living a happy life; it is not selfishness. The first step to developing resilience and finding true happiness is realizing and appreciating your own worth. Healthy, lasting connections with others are built on a foundation of self-love. Developing self-love improves empathy, communication, and the development of partnerships where both parties benefit.

Understanding Self-Love helps you better by guiding you toward self-acceptance, self-compassion, and positive self-image practices. Mindfulness, boundary-setting, and a positive outlook are strategies for cultivating self-love. Developing a healthy self-image requires deliberate work that includes embracing one's individuality and abilities.

Authenticity and sincere connections are fostered when vulnerability is embraced, which is a crucial component of self-love. Navigating vulnerability requires overcoming fear, embracing openness, and developing emotional resilience. Busting myths entails realizing that self-love is a deep respect for oneself rather than conceit. It embraces the inherent worth that every individual has and goes beyond affirmation from others. Taking the first steps toward self-love calls for perseverance, introspection, and a dedication to ongoing development.

Recall that loving oneself is a dynamic process rather than a destination. Appreciate the little things in life and show yourself self-compassion when you face obstacles. Effective communication, assertiveness training, and boundary-setting are all components of good relationships, which are linked to self-love. Authentic relationships are a result of letting go of expectations and developing an accepting mindset.

The cultivation of love and connection depends critically on mindfulness and presence. In partnerships, being really present improves communication and emotional kinship. Gratitude, introspection, and ongoing personal development are among the practices that help lay a solid basis for enduring love.

Overcoming barriers is a crucial component of success and personal development. Developing a positive outlook, establishing objectives, strengthening resilience, and taking lessons from failures are examples of strategies.

Inspiration and Motivation: These two dynamic forces are what propel the quest to "be the love you seek. Sustained personal development and relationship building need internalizing inspirational values and maintaining motivation.

Starting a self-love journey is a significant commitment to your health and the caliber of your relationships. Accept the process with open arms, understanding that each step no matter how tiny contributes to your personal development. Honor your accomplishments, draw lessons from setbacks, and develop self-compassion. Recall that the love you want originates from inside, and as you tend to it, you will genuinely spread that love outside into the world. I hope you find a lot of love along the way, as well as perseverance and self-discovery.

Printed in Great Britain
by Amazon

44502795R00059